The Convention People's Party Handbook

The Convention People's Party Handbook

The first fifty years
of Africa's
Revolutionary Party
1949–1999

Panaf
International Edition

CONVENTION PEOPLE'S PARTY HANDBOOK
INTERNATIONAL EDITION

Copyright © Panaf Books 2002

All rights reserved. No part of this publication may be reproduced, stored in any retrieval system, or tranmitted, in any form or by any means, electronic, mechanical, photocopying, recording or otherwise, without the prior permission in writing of Panaf Books, nor be otherwise circulated in any form of binding or cover other than that in which it is published and without a similar condition including this condition being imposed on subsequent purchaser.

ISBN 0 901787 59 0 [PB]

Panaf Books
75 Weston Street
London SE1 3RS

Foreword

When the Convention People's Party (CPP) was founded on 12 June 1949, its first task was to bring an end to colonial rule. For 'Ghana' was not yet born. It was the Gold Coast, a colony of Britain.

The roots of this great historic party lie as deep as the history of Ghana itself. Its foundation was the culmination of centuries of resistance to foreign exploitation.

There was never a time when colonialism went unchallenged. Nor a time since 1949 when the CPP has ceased to exist, in spite of its banning after the military coup of 24 February 1966.

A party whose time has come, firmly established in the hearts and minds of a people, never dies.

Contents

Preface

HISTORICAL BACKGROUND

Early times xi
The Bonds of 1844–45 xii
Indirect Rule xiii
Growing nationalist pressure
    for Self-Government xiv
The United Gold Coast Convention
    (UGCC) xvi
Ex-Servicemen's March xvii
Arrest of the 'Big Six' xviii

1 THE CONVENTION PEOPLE'S PARTY (CPP)

Birth of the CPP 1
CPP colours, motto and symbol 2
Structure 2
Membership 3
Policies (as stated in the CPP
    Constitution)
        National 4
        International 5

2 A PARTY OF THE PEOPLE: ELECTION VICTORIES

Building party support 7
Self-Government NOW 8

'*The Accra Evening News*' 9
Positive Action 10
Arrest of CPP leadership 12
1951 Election 12
The Motion of Destiny 14
1954 Election 14
1956 Election 15
Independence 6 March 1957 16

3 CPP GOVERNMENT 1957–66: BUILDING A NEW GHANA

The tasks ahead 19
Development Plans 19
Achievements 21
The Volta River Project (VRP) 22
Education 23
Women 24
Political education 24
Winneba Ideological Institute 25
Nkrumaism 26
The Republic of Ghana 27

4 CPP GOVERNMENT 1957-66: PAN-AFRICANISM — AN AFRICAN VOICE IN WORLD AFFAIRS

Pan-African Conferences 29
Steps towards African unification
   1. Ghana–Guinea Union,
      November 1958 31
   2. Ghana-Guinea-Mali Union,
      April 1961 31

    3. Ghana-Congo Agreement,
       August 1960 32
    4. The Organisation of African Unity
       (OAU), May 1963 32
African Personality 34
African Voice in World Affairs 35
Non-Aligned Movement 35
Afro-Asian solidarity 36
Organisation of Solidarity with the
    Peoples of Africa, Asia and
    Latin America (OSPAAL) 37
The CPP and the United Nations
    Organisation (UN) 38
The CPP and the Commonwealth 39
Hanoi peace mission 40

5   CPP IS BANNED:
THE CONAKRY YEARS 1966–72

End of CPP government 43
Villa Syli, Conakry 1966–72 45
CPP Overseas 48
External Nkrumaist groupings 48
The Party and Pan-Africanism 49
The death of Kwame Nkrumah 50
'Dark Days in Ghana' 51

6   CPP RENAISSANCE:
ACHIEVING NKRUMAIST UNITY

Problems of Nkrumaist parties and
    groupings 53
False dawns 55

People's Convention Party (PCP) 57
The Great Alliance 57
Memorandum of Understanding 59
Campaign to unban the CPP 59
The Convention Party (CP) 60
'The Convention' 61
Fiftieth birthday of the CPP:
    12th June 1999 62

Party Calendar 62

Books by Kwame Nkrumah 63

Chronology 65

Preface

HISTORICAL BACKGROUND

Early times

To set the CPP within its historical context, it is necessary to begin in the fifteenth century when the seeds of colonialism were sown in West Africa. It was a time when Portuguese seamen began to explore what was then known as the Guinea Coast. They discovered that the territory between the Ankobra and Volta rivers was rich in gold. They gave it the name 'El Mina' (the mine), soon to be called the Gold Coast.

Over the years other European seamen and traders entered into the scramble for West African trade. Forts and trading posts were built. The earliest English fort on the Gold Coast was Kormantine, built in 1631 but captured by the Dutch in 1665.

By the early sixteenth century, there was a flourishing trade between West Africa and Europe. Also, a lucrative trade in slaves to work on the plantations of America and the West Indies.

Elmina became the headquarters of Dutch merchants when they captured it from the Portuguese in 1637. The English-Royal Africa Company established its head quarters at Cape Coast castle, which was seized from the Dutch in 1664. The Dutch had ten other forts in the Gold Coast, the English nine others. Forts frequently changed hands as Europeans fought among themselves for ownership. From time to time there was also war among the various African peoples of the region, as well as between Africans and Europeans.

By the end of the eighteenth century, some 10,000 slaves a year were being exported from the Gold Coast, the majority by English merchants. Slavery was not abolished throughout the British empire until 1833.

By that time, the British had become the dominant European power in the Gold Coast, extending their influence from coastal areas far inland. At times they met with fierce resistance, notably from Ashanti. Dutch and Danish forts were taken over by the British. Gradually, and at first reluctantly, the British began to assume responsibility for the administration of conquered territory, though never claiming rights to the actual land.

The Bonds of 1844–45

The British negotiated a series of treaties known as 'Bonds' with African rulers in order to protect their trade. These treaties bound African chiefs to protect the rights of individuals and property in line with the general principles of English law. The territories of those who entered into Bonds were considered to form a British protectorate, as distinct from the coastal region which constituted a crown colony.

In the second half of the nineteenth century, relations between the British and the Ashantis deteriorated resulting in the Ashanti wars. It was not until 1896 that the Ashantis were finally defeated. The Asantehene, together with his leading supporters was deported to the Seychelles.

There followed the extension of British power north of Ashanti. In 1901, Orders in Council in Britain defined the boundaries of the Gold Coast Colony, Ashanti and the Northern Territories.

Indirect Rule

The British administered through the direct rule of British officials until there developed a system of indirect rule through District Officers, Legislative and Executive Councils working alongside traditional African authorities. Ultimate power, however, still rested in the Colonial Office and Parliament in London.

A Legislative Council was first established in the Gold Coast in 1850. It was empowered to make laws for the Colony with the Governor's consent. At first, members of both Legislative and Executive Councils were all British officials. But after a time, as a result of African nationalist pressure, it became the practice for the Governor to nominate a number of Africans to the Councils to represent local opinion.

Between 1922 and 1925, the Gold Coast constitution provided for the election of African legislative councillors. By 1945, the unofficial members of the Legislative Council outnumbered the official members. A measure of representative government, but not responsible government, had been achieved. For the Governor still remained responsible only to the British government in London.

The authority of the Legislative Council was originally limited to the Colony. Ashanti and the Northern Territories were administered by commissioners responsible to the Governor. In 1934, Ashanti was brought within the jurisdiction of the authorities in Accra. The Northern Territories followed a year later.

Growing nationalist pressure for Self-Government

During the first half of the twentieth century, rapidly growing discontent with colonial rule became well organised, drawing support from all sections of the population.

In the Gold Coast at this time were notable nationalists such as Dr Kwegyir Aggrey, Vice Principal of the Accra Training College when Kwame Nkrumah enrolled there in 1927. Aggrey regularly addressed huge audiences in Accra, inspiring the people to assert their right to self-government.

The message Aggrey preached was spread through newspapers such as the *African Morning Post* edited by the Nigerian nationalist Nnamdi Azikwe (ZIK). Another newspaper, the *African Sentinel* edited by the Sierra Leonian, Wallace Johnson, also vehemently attacked racialism and colonialism.

In 1933, Wallace Johnson with Bankole Awooner-Renner, Wuta-Ofei and others founded the West African Youth League (WAYL), branches of which came to be established throughout the country.

Further impetus for national liberation was provided through the activities of the national Congress of British West Africa (NCBWA), founded in 1920, to campaign for political, economic and social reform in all the colonial territories of West Africa. The Gold Coast lawyer, J. E. Casely Hayford was a founder member. The NCBWA filled the gap left by the declining influence of the Aborigines Protection Society (ARPS), formed in 1897 and regarded as the first organisation of its kind to campaign for the rights of Africans.

The ever-growing pressure for self-government compelled Britain to allow limited constitutional reform. Under the Burns constitution, Africans were appointed for the first time to the Gold Coast Executive, and there was an African majority in the Legislative Council. There were at that time two parties, the Gold Coast People's League and the Gold Coast National Party.

The United Gold Coast Convention (UGCC)

At an historic meeting in Saltpond on 4 August 1947, the two parties united to form the UGCC. Leading figures in the Convention were J. B. Danquah, William Ofori Atta, Akufo Addo, J. W. de Graft Johnson and V. B. Annan. Pa Grant was elected chairman.

The UGCC represented mainly members of the professional and business class. To be effective, the Convention needed to widen support to include ordinary people, particularly the young who were becoming impatient with the slow pace of change.

It was decided to invite Kwame Nkrumah, a political activist then in London, to become general secretary of the UGCC. Nkrumah had a wide reputation as an experienced political organiser with a gift for leadership. Together with George Padmore and others he had organised in 1945 the Fifth Pan-African Congress in Manchester, England. Nkrumah personally drew up the dynamic *Declaration to the Colonial Peoples of the World*, approved and adopted by the Congress. He was an eminently suitable person to galvanise the mass of the Gold Coast people and the youth to play an active part in the national liberation movement.

Nkrumah was hesitant about accepting the position, being aware that both the composition and objectives of the UGCC fell far short of the radical, political programme he envisaged for the Gold Coast and for Africa. But after discussion with his colleagues he decided to accept, knowing that it might not be long before he would find it impossible to continue working within the UGCC.

Nkrumah arrived back in the Gold Coast on 16 December 1947. Within the next two years he achieved a remarkable transformation of the nationalist movement. In 1947 there were only two branches of the UGCC. By 1949 branches had been formed in towns and villages throughout the country. Organisations such as the trade unions, cooperative societies, women's and youth groups, farmers councils and ex-servicemen were drawn into the campaign. Through leadership and meticulous organisation at every level, Nkrumah mobilised the previously politically unheard people into militant participation in the struggle. Everywhere, the liberation message was spread, that only independence could bring improvement in living conditions.

The UGCC founders insisted the campaign be non-violent, proceeding step by step to achieve self-government in the shortest possible time.

Ex-Servicemen's March

A crucial point was reached on 20 February 1948 when both Nkrumah and Danquah spoke at a rally of ex-servicemen in Accra. A petition expressing their grievances was drawn up to be presented to the Governor.

On 28 February the ex-servicemen set off to march to Christiansborg Castle to present their petition. Their way was blocked by armed police commanded by a British officer, Superintendent Colin Imray.

When the marchers refused to halt, Imray gave the order to open fire. Three ex-servicemen were killed. Others were injured.

News of the shooting sparked off days of rioting in Accra by already angry crowds incensed at the high price of food, which they blamed on the greed of foreign merchants. Shops and offices owned by foreigners were attacked and looted. Violence spread to other towns.

Faced with widespread disorder, the Governor, Sir Gerald Creasy, declared a state of emergency. Troops were called out while police arrested so-called trouble makers.

The Executive Committee of the UGCC sent telegrams to A. Creech Jones, British Secretary of State for the Colonies, asking for a Special Commissioner to be sent to the Gold Coast with power to call a Constituent Assembly.

Arrest of the 'Big Six'

There followed the arrest of the leaders of the UGCC — J. B. Danquah, Ofori Atta, Akufo Addo, Ako Adjei, Obetsebi Lamptey and Kwame Nkrumah. They were flown to the Northern Territories where they were detained for six weeks before being taken to Accra to appear at a Commission of Enquiry set up by the Governor under the chairmanship of Aiken Watson Q.C.

After interrogating the accused, the Watson commissioners concluded Nkrumah was mainly to blame for the disorders. In their words: 'The UGCC did not really get down to business until the arrival of Mr Nkrumah on 16 December 1947'. They correctly detected that Nkrumah's political objectives were far more progressive than those of his colleagues. They recommended the drafting of a new constitution to replace the outdated Burns constitution. As a result, in December 1948, a constitutional committee was appointed by the Governor under the chairmanship of Mr Justice Coussey.

By then it was clear that differences between Nkrumah and other leaders of the UGCC would soon make it impossible for them to continue to work together. Danquah and his colleagues had become alarmed at the rapidly growing support of their members for Nkrumah and his dynamic leadership. They disapproved of his founding of the Committee on Youth Organisation (CYO), regarding it as a pressure group advancing Nkrumah's determination to speed up the campaign for self-government. The CYO adopted the slogan 'Self-Government Now', in contrast to the UGCC slogan 'Self-Government in the shortest possible time'. They feared Nkrumah's policy might lead to further disorder and further arrests. Meantime, Nkrumah and his supporters became increasingly exasperated at what they saw as the timidity of the UGCC.

By mid-1949, with the mass of the people and the youth behind him, Nkrumah and his colleagues were in a strong position to split with the UGCC to form a new party.

1

THE CONVENTION PEOPLE'S PARTY (CPP)

Birth of the CPP

The CPP was born in Accra on the 12th of June 1949, before a crowd of some 60,000 people which had gathered on the Old Polo Ground. On that day, Kwame Nkrumah resigned as general secretary of the UGCC, and declared that the CYO had decided to break away from the UGCC to become an entirely separate political party, the CPP. The decision to form a new party had been taken a few days before at a special conference of the CYO held in Tarkwa.

The foundation of the CPP marked a decisive turning point in the history of Ghana. For it led directly to the achievement of Ghana's independence on 6 March 1957.

CPP colours, motto and symbol

The colours of the party were to be red, white and green, the tricolour flag in horizontal form with red at the top, white in the centre and green at the bottom. Party motto:

> FORWARD, EVER
> BACKWARD NEVER

Its symbol: A red cockerel heralding the dawn.

Structure

Party branches were to be established in every town and village, throughout the country. It was to be a mass based party each branch of which was to be administered by an elected Branch Executive Committee. There was to be a National Secretariat under the direct supervision and control of the Central Committee of the Party.

Members of the first Central Committee were:

> Kwame Nkrumah (Chairman)
> Kojo Botsio (Secretary)
> K. A. Gbedemah
> N. A. Welbeck
> Kwesi Plange
> Kofi Baako
> Krobo Edusei
> Dzenkle Dzewu
> Ashie Nikoi

1 The Convention People's Party (CPP)

Membership

1. Individual. Open to any person over 18 years of age.
2. Affiliated.
   — Trade Unions
   — Ex-Servicemen's Union
   — Farmers' organisations
   — Cooperative societies
   — Organisations of professionals, artisans and technicians

- Youth and sports organisations
- Women's' organisations
- Other organisations approved by CPP National Executive

Both individual and affiliated members had to accept the objectives and discipline of the Party.

Policies (as stated in the CPP Constitution)

National

(1) To fight relentlessly to achieve and maintain independence of the people of Ghana (Gold Coast) and their chiefs.

(2) To serve as the vigorous conscious political vanguard for removing all forms of oppression and for the establishment of a democratic government.

(3) To secure and maintain the complete unity of the people of the Colony, Ashanti, Northern Territories and Trans-Volta/Togoland regions.

(4) To work with and in the interest of the Trade Union Movement, and other kindred organisations, in joint political or other action in harmony with the constitution and Standing Orders of the Party.

(5) To work for a speedy reconstruction of a better Ghana (Gold Coast) in which the people and their Chiefs shall have the right to live and govern themselves as free people.

(6) To promote the Political, Social and Economic emancipation of the people, more particularly of those who depend directly, upon their own exertions by hand or by brain for the means of life.

International

(1) To work with other nationalist democratic and socialist movements in Africa and other continents, with a view to abolishing imperialism, colonialism, racialism, tribalism and all forms of national and racial oppression and economic inequality among nations, races and peoples and to support all action for World Peace.

(2) To support the demand for a West African Federation and of PanAfricanism by promoting unity of action among the peoples of Africa and of African descent.

Basic principles and strategy of CPP policies, stated in the party constitution, have endured, though at times it became necessary to develop and adapt them to changing circumstances.

2

A PARTY OF THE PEOPLE: ELECTION VICTORIES

Building party support

In the early days of the CPP, and frequently afterwards, Nkrumah urged party activists to:

> 'Go to the people
> Live among them
> Learn from them
> Love them
> Serve them
> Plan with them
> Start with what they know
> Build on what they have.'

This was sound Maoist advice for the building of any nationalist, progressive party, and very suited to the organisation and policies of the CPP. In the words of Nkrumah: 'The masses of the people form the backbone of our Party. Their living conditions and their welfare must be paramount in everything we do. It is for them in particular, and Africa in general, that our Party exists.'

For the first time, through the various democratic organs of the CPP, the people were empowered.

Decisions of the Party were those of the entire membership. At party meetings and rallies, policies were clearly stated and discussed. All were encouraged to express their views. The gatherings were joyful occasions, the political messages of the CPP being regarded as cause for celebration. The most humble were made to feel important by being given the opportunity to participate in the freeing of their country.

Through the process of enrolment as a party member, people felt they belonged to a countrywide movement with objectives which would make a real difference to their lives.

The use of slogans, party songs and symbols, constantly used and publicised, helped to spread the party message that only independence could bring about an improvement in living conditions.

With amazing speed, CPP branches were formed in towns, villages and places of work throughout the country. Each branch had an elected Branch Executive Committee, linked to regional and central authorities, thereby ensuring a two-way process of consultation.

Self-Government NOW

Between 1949 and 1957 the CPP concentrated on achieving its first objective, the winning of

2 A Party of the People: Election Victories

independence. For until political freedom was attained, the Party could not implement long-term objectives of socialist planning and Pan-African goals.

'The Accra Evening News'

In the days of no TV and limited radio, publicity for a Party campaign depended largely on the spoken and written word, newspapers, placards, posters, pamphlets and so on. The written word was of special importance. Nkrumah considered it an essential component of political struggle.

The CPP had, in Nkrumah, not only a highly gifted speaker, but an experienced political writer. During the ten years (1937–47) he had spent studying and working in the USA and Britain, he had edited numerous campaigning newspapers and journals.

The CPP's campaign was brilliantly publicised in the party's first newspaper, *The Accra Evening News*, founded by Nkrumah in 1948, the first issue of which appeared on 3 September.

Each day, through the columns of this paper the CPP's political agenda was publicised; the injustices of colonialism exposed and Pan-African objectives promulgated.

The paper became so popular that it was sometimes impossible to satisfy demand because of lack of funds and limited printing capacity. Copies of the paper would be shared among many readers.

Its famous mottoes headed each issue:

— *We have the right to live as men*

— *We prefer self-government with danger to servitude in tranquillity*

— *We have the right to govern ourselves*

Soon, 'Self-government NOW' as well as other slogans printed in the newspaper began to appear on walls and buildings throughout the country.

When *The Accra Evening News* was founded, Nkrumah had already written his first book *Towards Colonial Freedom*. He was to write fifteen more, and several pamphlets.

Positive Action

The CPP was ready when the Report of the Coussey Committee was published in October 1949. Anticipating that its constitutional proposals would be unacceptable, plans had been made for Positive Action.

Nkrumah explained what was meant by Positive Action in a statement written in 1949 entitled *What I mean by Positive Action*. He listed the weapons of Positive Action as:

1. Legitimate political agitation
2. Newspaper and educational campaigns
3. As a last resort, the constitutional application of strikes, boycotts, and non-cooperation based on the principle of absolute non-violence.

2 A Party of the People: Election Victories

The final stage of Positive Action would only be employed if all other avenues to achieve self-government had been closed.

As expected, the Coussey Committee's constitutional proposals provided for very limited African participation in government.

The CPP organised the summoning of a Ghana People's Representative Assembly. The Assembly passed a resolution declaring the Coussey proposals unacceptable, and proposing amendments.

On 15 December, the Executive Committee of the CPP informed the Governor, Sir Charles Arden-Clarke, that unless the legitimate aspirations of the people as embodied in the proposed amendments to the Coussey Committee's report were accepted, the CPP would declare Positive Action. The Governor was given two weeks in which to accede to the CPP's request for the calling of a Constituent Assembly.

A wave of arrests followed. Editors of newspapers founded by Nkrumah were imprisoned. Nkrumah was charged with contempt for an article which appeared in the *Sekondi Morning Telegraph*.

After several meetings with the colonial authorities, it was clear that no Constituent Assembly would be called. Nkrumah, therefore, on 8 January 1950 proclaimed Positive Action. He then went to Cape Coast, Sekondi and Tarkwa to declare that Positive Action had begun. He called for a general strike to include all except those engaged in maintaining essential services such as hospitals and water supplies. Shops and offices closed. Road and rail services came to a standstill.

The colonial government responded on 10 January by declaring a state of emergency. The offices of CPP newspapers were raided and closed.

Arrest of CPP leadership

By 22 January 1950, all CPP leaders had been arrested. Nkrumah was taken to James Fort prison in Accra, charged with inciting people to take part in an illegal strike in an attempt to coerce the government. He was found guilty and sentenced to three years' imprisonment. Things would never be the same again. The CPP had shown that an unarmed people *could* demonstrate the effectiveness of unified effort in the form of Positive Action. Never again would they accept that it was hopeless to challenge a seemingly mighty power structure. The political revolution in the Gold Coast had begun in earnest.

1951 Election

There were three landslide CPP election victories in the years leading up to independence. The first was held in February 1951 while Nkrumah was in James Fort. From prison he stood as official CPP candidate for the Accra Central constituency, conducting the election campaign from his prison cell. He was helped by a friendly warder who managed to smuggle messages to party headquarters, where the work of the CPP was continuing. A concise CPP election manifesto, written on sheets of toilet paper, was delivered to CPP/HQ in this way.

2 A Party of the People: Election Victories

CPP manifestos were always short, simple and direct, leaving the electorate in no doubt about what a CPP victory would mean. They expressed just what the majority of the people wanted. As election results showed, the CPP correctly gauged the pulse of the nation.

In 1951 the manifesto could be summed up in three words: Self-Government NOW.

The election result was a resounding victory for the CPP. The Party won 34 out of a possible 38 elected seats, and had a majority in the Assembly over the nominated members. Nkrumah was elected for Accra Central with 22,780 votes from a possible 23,122, the largest individual poll so far recorded.

Faced with this result, the Governor was compelled to release Nkrumah from prison to become Leader of Government Business.

In the following years the CPP kept up pressure on the colonial government. While Africans had a majority in the Assembly and the Executive Council, the ex-officio members appointed by the Governor controlled the key areas of defence, external affairs, finance and justice. They held the real reins of power. In addition, the Governor retained the power to veto any legislation and the authority to prorogue or dissolve parliament. It was a situation which the CPP was not prepared to tolerate.

On 5 March 1952, Nkrumah's position as Leader of Government Business disappeared from the constitution, the office of Prime Minister replacing it.

Nkrumah, as leader of the CPP, became the first African prime minister.

The way had been cleared for the final steps to be taken towards Independence. There were eight Ghanaians in the Cabinet of eleven, but still the Governor's nominees held the key ministries.

The Motion of Destiny

On 10 July 1953, Nkrumah introduced into the Assembly the historic Motion of Destiny. This called upon Britain to make arrangements for Independence. It required all members of the Assembly to be elected directly by secret ballot, and Cabinet members to be members of the Assembly and directly responsible to it. Britain was asked for a clear commitment to Independence by naming a date.

Britain conceded the demand for Independence but insisted on another election first.

The CPP was confident of another convincing win, in spite of opposition elements which had regrouped. Against the CPP demand for Self-Government 'Now', they stood for Self-Government 'Soon'.

1954 Election

In this election, the CPP won 72 out of 104 seats in the Assembly. The second largest group were the independents. It was only in the Northern Territories that the CPP failed to obtain a majority. As before, the CPP emerged as the only truly national party with 38 seats in the Colony, 18 in Ashanti, 8 in Trans-Volta, 8 in the Northern Territories.

2 A Party of the People: Election Victories

The election gave the country its first All-African Assembly.

Once again, the colonial government was faced with a clear verdict of the people. But it was still unwilling to name a date for Independence. Its policy of delay was helped by anti-CPP forces which had emerged under a new name, the National Liberation Movement (NLM). This drew most of its strength from Ashanti. The Asanteman Council, headed by the Asantehene, joined with the NLM to campaign for a federal form of government, enabling Ashanti to manage its own affairs.

1956 Election

For a time after the 1954 election, the rate of progress slowed while the CPP and the NLM contested the question of whether Ghana should be a unitary or a federalist state. Violence erupted in parts of the country, giving Britain a further excuse to delay matters, by demanding yet another general election before granting Independence.

The CPP election machine sprang into action, confident of a decisive result but taking no chances.

As on previous occasions, the party manifesto was brief, summed up in just seventeen words:

> *'Do I want Independence in my lifetime? Or do I want to revert to feudalism and imperialism?'*

The impractical, divisive option of federalism in a country the size of Ghana was not allowed to cloud the issue.

The election was another great victory for the CPP. The Party won 71 seats, later increased by the support of one of the Independents, giving the CPP a majority of 40 in the Assembly.

Again, support came from every region of the country. Even in Ashanti, the stronghold of the NLM, the CPP gained 43 per cent of the total votes cast.

On 17 September 1956, in response to a formal request from the CPP to the British Secretary of State to name a firm date for Independence, the Governor informed Nkrumah that 6 March 1957 had been decided upon. Amid scenes of great jubilation, the news was given to the Assembly by Nkrumah on the following day, 18 September 1956.

Independence 6 March 1957

At midnight on 5/6 March 1957, on the Polo Ground in Accra, Nkrumah proclaimed the Independence of Ghana. To cries of *FREEDOM!, FREEDOM!, FREEDOM!* from the huge crowd the British flag was lowered, and the red, green and gold flag of Ghana was raised in its place.

It was the climax of the CPP's epic campaign to bring colonial rule to an end.

The Party's first objective, the battle for political freedom had been won, without resort to arms. In the words of Nkrumah on that historic night:

2 A Party of the People: Election Victories

'At long last the battle has ended. And thus Ghana, your beloved country is free for ever'.

But there would be further battles in the years ahead to build a new Ghana and to achieve Pan-African objectives. The struggle for economic independence and social justice was only just beginning. In the wider context, the CPP's Pan-African policy was expressed in the famous words of Nkrumah at the end of his midnight speech at Independence:

'The Independence of Ghana is meaningless unless it is linked up with the total liberation of the African continent'.

3

CPP GOVERNMENT 1957–66: BUILDING A NEW GHANA

The tasks ahead

With Independence, the CPP government at last had the political power needed to build the economic and social infrastructure necessary for Ghana to become a modern, progressive state.

The Party inherited an economy developed mainly to serve foreign interests. Education, health and other social needs of the people, though improved with the implementation of the CPP's first Development Plan (1951-6), still fell far below the high standards at which the CPP aimed.

Much remained to be done.

Development Plans

Through Development Plans the Party was determined to restructure the economy so that the people, through the state would have an effective share in the economy of the country and effective control over it. The needs of the people and not so-called market principles would be the paramount consideration in economic planning.

The Consolidation Plan (1957–9), covered the first two years of Independence, giving time for the government to consolidate in preparation for the launching of a far-reaching Five Year Development Plan (1959-64).

All sections of the community had a part to play in the economic and social revolution. The CPP entered into a Grand Alliance with the Trade Union Congress (TUC) and the Ghana Farmers' council. CPP Ministers, Ministerial Secretaries and others were directed by the Central Committee of the CPP to give up ten per cent of their salaries.

As Nkrumah stated:

> 'We are now working for Ghana regardless of party affiliations. The government will see to it that any sacrifices which the workers, whether by hand or brain, and the farmers may make, will not rob them of the fruits of their labour. The government will ensure that these sacrifices will be made for the benefit of all the people. '

In 1962, the CPP Programme for Work and Happiness was proclaimed, furthering the Party's development policies based on socialist principles.

Then in March 1964, building on the work of previous Plans, the Seven Year Development Plan was launched. The main tasks of the Plan were to:

3 CPP Government 1957–66: Building A New Ghana

1. Speed up the growth of the national economy.
2. Embark upon the socialist transformation of the economy through the rapid development of state and co-operative sectors.
3. Eradicate completely the colonial structure of the economy.

There was to be a period of mixed economy, when a limited private sector would be allowed to operate. During this time, public and co-operative sectors would expand rapidly, particularly in the strategic, productive sectors of the economy.

Eventually, with the complete implementation of Development Plans, a fully planned economy and a just society would be established.

Achievements

During the period of CPP government, the standard of living of the people was greatly enhanced. Houses, schools, clinics, hospitals, were opened. A network of roads, considered among the best in Africa were constructed. A piped water supply was provided to villages which had never before enjoyed such an amenity. Many state enterprises and corporations were set up, supervised by a State Management Committee.

Among new industries founded were two cocoa processing plants, two sugar refineries, a textile printing plant, a glass factory, a chocolate factory, a meat processing plant, and a large printing works at Tema. In addition, work was far advanced on a gold refinery at Tarkwa, cement, shoe and rubber tyre factories at Kumasi, and a factory for the manufacture of pre-fabricated houses. Ghana was beginning to supply local demand for many basic consumer goods, using locally produced raw materials.

The harbour at Takoradi was extended. An entirely new artificial harbour was constructed at Tema with a dual carriageway to connect the new town and port of Tema with Accra.

Communications of all kinds, telephone, radio, newspapers were developed. Ghana had its own shipping line, the Black Star Line; also its own airline, Ghana Airways. Plans were advanced for the transformation of Accra airport to bring it up to international standards.

The Ghana navy and Air Force owe their origins to the CPP government.

Great strides were made to modernise and diversify agriculture, breaking away from the limited, colonial pattern of a single crop economy. The CPP's agricultural policy aimed to provide the nation's food, and also the needs of industry.

State farms cultivated rubber, oil palm, banana, citrus fruits and other crops. Canning and processing plants were built. The agricultural wing of the Workers' Brigade alone farmed some 12,500 acres of cereals and vegetables. Ghana's forests supplied timber for a growing furniture industry and for export.

The Volta River Project (VRP)

CPP plans for industrialisation and radical social

reform involved the production of hydro-electric power on a massive scale. It was the purpose of the VRP to provide this power with enough capacity to spare for export to neighbouring states.

Ghana was estimated to have sufficient bauxite to last for 200 years. It was the intention to process this through an alumina plant at Tema using hydro-electric power from the Dam at Akosombo.

The Volta Dam was officially opened by Nkrumah on 23 January 1966. He described it as 'the greatest of all our development projects'.

Education

The 1961 Education Act made education compulsory for all school-age children, boys and girls.

Education from primary to university level was made free. Textbooks were supplied free to pupils in primary, middle and secondary schools.

New schools and colleges were opened. The University College of the Gold Coast became the University of Ghana, enlarged with new faculties more suited to meet the needs of a rapidly developing independent state. From Achimota the University moved to Legon where an entirely new university campus had been built. Staff in the Extra-Mural Department travelled the country bringing higher education to those whose studies had ceased with leaving school.

The economic development plans of the Party required skilled scientists and technicians. These were trained in the Kumasi College of Technology, later to become the University of Science and Technology.

By 1966, Ghana had one of the highest literacy rates in Africa and among the best public services.

Women

It was CPP policy to advance the role of women in nation building.

The National Council of Ghana Women (NCGW) was inaugurated by Nkrumah on 10 September 1960 as an integral wing of the CPP. The NCGW, with branches throughout the country, was represented on the Central Committee of the Party.

Discriminatory provisions relating to women's work were abolished. Equal pay was instituted for equal work. Maternity leave on full pay was assured.

Ten women parliamentarians took their seats in the parliament of 1961. Women were appointed to serve on the boards of corporations, schools and town councils.

Women underwent pilot training in the Ghana Air Force Training School at Takoradi and were encouraged to enrol in the army to train alongside men in the infantry, intelligence services and to become electrical and mechanical engineers.

Political education

The CPP, a mass-based party, had won political power through the ballot box mainly on the relatively simple issue of ending colonial rule.

3 CPP Government 1957–66: Building A New Ghana

After Independence, the great task of economic and social reconstruction required a people politically aware of the challenges ahead, and of their role in meeting them. An in-depth programme of political education was needed.

In 1958 the Ghana Young Pioneer Movement was founded. The purpose was to widen the school curriculum to include political education to equip pupils to grow into aware, responsible citizens. Through activities and training, Young Pioneers were to learn about CPP policies and Pan-African objectives. It became compulsory for each pupil to join the Movement and to pledge loyalty to it.

The National African Students' Organisation (NASSO) was another means by which the CPP drew the youth into the forefront of the struggle to build the new Ghana.

NASSO study groups were organised to spread the political education of the people.

As a result of its work, and the efforts of party Vanguard Activists, the general level of political awareness was considerably raised.

Winneba Ideological Institute

The Institute was founded in 1961 'to provide a steady flow of ideologically sound cadres to carry on the work of politicisation.' It became a centre where party members from the Central Committee to local official level could undergo courses of study, and hold discussions on party organisation and objectives.

The Institute comprised two sections:
1. Ideological training centre
2. Positive Action training centre.

There was no excuse for any party member who had passed through a course at Winneba not to know party policies.

The reputation of Winneba attracted students from most parts of Africa and beyond.

Nkrumaism

Ghana, during the time of the CPP government, experienced the ideology of Nkrumaism in practice. For Nkrumaism embodies CPP fundamental principles and provides a practical guide for action.

It is not a static, rigid set of rules, but a living ideology, born and bred in Africa, evolved through years of struggle and experience. Its strategy is consistent, to develop Africa's immense human and natural resources to the full for the benefit of the peoples of Africa. But it is tactically flexible to meet the challenges of changing circumstances. It may be summed up in three words: Liberation, Justice, Unity.

In Ghana it was publicised in the press, notably in *The Spark*, the CPP's theoretical journal. Editors of the paper published the booklet *Some Essential Features of Nkrumaism* in 1964. It was based on articles which had appeared in the paper.

Nkrumah's books, *I Speak of Freedom* (1961), *Africa Must Unite* (1963), and *Consciencism* (1964) had by

3 CPP Government 1957–66: Building A New Ghana

then been published. *Neocolonialism: The Last Stage of Imperialism* (1965) and *Challenge of the Congo* (1967) were in preparation. Each book written by Nkrumah were expressions of Nkrumaism, the shared political programme of Nkrumah and the CPP.

The Republic of Ghana

Three years after Independence, in March 1960, proposals for a republican constitution were published. A plebiscite was then held in April, the result of which made it clear that the people of Ghana welcomed a republican constitution, and overwhelmingly voted for Nkrumah to become the first President.

On 1 July 1960, Ghana became a Republic. The Governor General, Lord Listowel, performed his last duty, the prorogation of Parliament.

The Republican constitution contained the unique provision that:

'The independence of Ghana should not be surrendered or diminished on any grounds other than the furtherance of African unity, that no person would suffer discrimination on grounds of sex, race, tribe, religion or political belief, and that chieftaincy in Ghana would be guaranteed and preserved. Freedom and justice would be honoured and maintained'.

Nkrumah was installed as President at State House on 1 July 1960.

On that same day, the new President, accompanied by President Sékou Touré of Guinea and other African leaders, lit the flame of African freedom. This was to be kept burning to symbolise the CPP government's continuing, vigorous Pan-African efforts to bring about the total liberation and unity of the continent.

4

CPP GOVERNMENT 1957-66: PAN-AFRICANISM — AN AFRICAN VOICE IN WORLD AFFAIRS

Pan-African Conferences

With Independence, the Party was in a position to embark on a practical programme of Pan-Africanism. This involved meaningful support for Africa's freedom fighters and the taking of effective steps to advance African unity.

In 1957, there were only eight independent African states. They were Ghana, Ethiopia, Libya, Tunisia, Morocco, Egypt, Liberia and Sudan. Most of the African continent was yet to be liberated. The last Pan-African Congress had been held in Manchester, England in 1945.

The CPP government was determined to reactivate the Pan-African Movement on the soil of Africa its true home. Practical steps were taken.

1. In April 1958 the Conference of African Independent States was held in Accra. The eight states agreed to co-ordinate economic planning; to

improve communications; to exchange cultural and educational information; to assist liberation movements by providing training and other facilities.

Most important was the adoption of the formula of one man one vote as an objective of the liberation movement. This gave the liberation movement direction and cohesion.

2. In December 1958, the All-African People's Conference was held in Accra. This Conference represented Africa's freedom fighters, nationalist parties, trade unions, co-operative and youth movements throughout Africa. It was the first time that freedom fighters from British, French, Portuguese, Spanish and racist minority regimes had met together to discuss common problems and to formulate plans. History was made when the Conference endorsed the right of the unliberated to use all methods of struggle, including armed struggle, if non-violent methods to obtain freedom had failed.

At the Conference were Patrice Lumumba, Kenneth Kaunda, Kanyama Chiume, Tom Mboya, Oginga Odinga, Joshua Nkomo and many others who were to become notable political leaders.

Conference members returned to their countries with a common purpose to liberate their countries. They were inspired as never before, and confident in the CPP government's commitment to the Pan-African struggle. On obtaining independence, they were to follow Ghana's example in making their territories base areas for freedom fighters. Ghana had become the pace-maker of the Pan-African Movement.

3. Among liberation movements which received aid and training in Ghana during the government of the CPP were:
- ANC (African National Congress)
- PAC (Pan-African Congress)
- ZANU (Zimbabwe African National Union)
- ZAPU (Zimbabwe African People's Union)
- MPLA (Popular Movement for the Liberation of Angola
- SWAPO (South West African People's Organisation
- FRELIMO (Front for the Liberation of Mozambique)

Steps towards African unification

1. Ghana–Guinea Union, November 1958

This was to mark the start of the actual process of unification by setting up a nucleus union which other states could join as and when they wished. The CPP and the PDG (Parti Démocratique de Guinée) shared the same Pan-African objectives, and followed a similar path of social and economic development.

2. Ghana-Guinea-Mali Union, April 1961

This was formed when President Modibo Keita of Mali joined President Sékou Touré of Guinea and President Nkrumah in Accra and agreed on a Charter for the Union of African States (UAS) which was open to other states to join. The UAS reaffirmed support for the liberation movement and agreed that an African Common Market should be formed.

3. Ghana-Congo Agreement, August 1960

The outcome of a secret meeting in Accra between Nkrumah and Patrice Lumumba, then prime minister of the Congo. They agreed to form a political union, a republican constitution within a federal framework. The capital to be Kinshasa (then Leopoldville).

The Agreement was never implemented because of the fall of Lumumba's government the following month and his subsequent assassination.

The CPP government, throughout its tenure of power, demonstrated time and again the possibility of achieving a degree of unity between states with differing historical backgrounds, language, culture and institutions. As expressed by Nkrumah:

> 'The forces that unite us are intrinsic, and greater than the superimposed influences that keep us apart. It is not just our colonial past, or the fact that we have aims in common. It is something which goes far deeper. I can best describe it as a sense of oneness in that we are *Africans.*'

4. The Organisation of African Unity (OAU), May 1963

The foundation of the OAU was the culmination of the CPP government's initiative to establish political machinery for the unification of Africa.

The Charter of the OAU was signed in Addis Ababa on 25 May 1963 by the Heads of State and Governments of 32 African independent states.

All the signatories were agreed on the principles of African liberation and unity. But they differed on questions of procedure and priorities. While some advocated a gradualist approach, emphasis being on economic, cultural and regional groupings, others led by Ghana considered it essential to provide political machinery to plan liberation and development on a continental scale. It was consistently the Party view that Africa's huge natural and human resources could only be developed to the full for the well-being of the African people as a whole if Africa was united.

These differences and the lack of provision for an All-African High Command to provide strength to enforce OAU decisions, meant that the Charter was one of intent rather than of positive action.

Later OAU Summit Conferences also failed to agree the setting up of effective political machinery.

The final OAU Summit held during the period of CPP government was in Accra in 1965. The Party's attempt to establish a full-time OAU Executive Council narrowly failed to obtain the required number of votes.

Nkrumah predicted that the continued failure of Africa to unite would mean 'stagnation, instability and confusion, making Africa an easy prey to foreign interference and confusion'. He warned that the independent states would be 'picked off one by one'. As he remarked in 1965 'It is courage that we lack'.

African Personality

The concept of the African Personality is an important aspect of CPP thinking. Nkrumah described it as a 'reawakening consciousness among Africans and peoples of African descent of the bonds which unite us — our historical past, our culture, our common experience and our aspirations'. It was expressed by the CPP government through:

a) Africanisation to break down old colonial structures and personnel in the civil service, armed forces and police. To eradicate the 'colonial mentality'. It was not based on racism. Foreigners were welcomed to work in Ghana provided they were sincerely committed to CPP objectives.

b) Bureau of African Affairs in Accra set up to administer to the needs of Africa's freedom fighters.

c) Institute of African Studies opened in 1963 as part of the University of Ghana. Attached to the Institute was the School of Performing Arts. A Dance Ensemble and a national Orchestra were formed to express both modern and traditional culture.

d) First Africanist Conference in Accra 1962 to plan a comprehensive programme of research into all aspects of Africa's history, culture, thought and human and material resources. Results of research to be published in an Encyclopedia Africana. Eminent US scholars Dr W. E. B.

DuBois and Dr W. Alphaeus Hunton were invited to Ghana to work on the project.

e) Links with peoples of African descent in the Diaspora. Ghana during the time of the CPP government was described as 'the very fountainhead of Pan-Africanism'. (Malcolm X after a visit to Ghana in 1964)

f) George Padmore Research Library on African Affairs opened in Accra in 1961

African Voice in World Affairs

The emergence of a distinctive African voice in world affairs was something new in international relations. It was another direct result of CPP policy after Independence, which generated a remarkable succession of developments throughout Africa and the Diaspora.

Africans were no longer prepared to be silent spectators in world affairs.

Non-Aligned Movement

Ghana and African countries which obtained independence soon after emerged on the world political scene when the 'cold war' between the USA and the USSR dominated international affairs. The nuclear arms race was at its height. The world seemed on the brink of war.

The Non-Aligned Movement offered hope of a Third Force holding the balance of power and thus avoiding war. In this political climate, newly-independent states of Africa and Asia adopted a non-aligned stand.

Economic development requirements necessitated reasonably good relations with both sides in the 'cold war'. By acting together the mainly former colonial peoples of the world could carry some weight internationally.

The spirit of solidarity took form at the Bandung Conference in 1955, when the peoples of Africa and Asia, together with representatives of liberation movements, met for the first time to discuss common problems.

Among the most notable leaders of the Non-Aligned Movement were President Nkrumah representing the CPP government, President Jawaharlal Nehru of India, President Abdul Nasser of Egypt, President Tito of Yugoslavia and President Sukarno of Indonesia.

Conferences of Non-Aligned States were held in Belgrade (1961), Cairo (1964) and elsewhere in subsequent years. However, in the changing political climate, non-alignment was to become in the view of Nkrumah 'an anachronism'.

Afro-Asian solidarity

This was more than a political expression. It implied the solidarity of peoples as well as of governments. Afro-Asian co-operation meant the development of a common political and economic strategy, the organising of associations, the exchange of students and other ways of strengthening bonds of friendship between the peoples of Africa and Asia.

In May 1965, the CPP government hosted the 4th Afro-Asian Solidarity Conference. In the words of Nkrumah:

> 'Let no-one mistake this as a racial alignment...We are here because we are resolved that any system or regime which owes its existence to the exploitation of man by man, cannot and must not be permitted to continue its existence in the world.'

He emphasised how much more effective Africa's human and material resources would be when mobilised under a continental Union Government.

Organisation of Solidarity with the Peoples of Africa, Asia and Latin America (OSPAAL)

Nkrumah, Ben Barka, leading Moroccan opposition figure, and Fidel Castro were responsible for the formation of OSPAAL. A need was felt for an organisation independent of both the USSR and China. At that time, relations between China and the USSR were very strained.

The OSPAAL journal *Tricontinental* was published from the organisation's headquarters in Cuba.

Ben Barka was a frequent guest of the CPP government. Sadly, shortly after OSPAAL was formed, he was assassinated.

The CPP and the United Nations Organisation (UN)

The emergence of a meaningful African voice in the largest of international bodies, the UN, may be traced to the period of the CPP government.

It was the gaining of independence by so many African countries after Ghana's example in 1957, that African membership of the UN increased dramatically.

Previously, the presence of the few African states had scarcely been noticed. They shared no common policy, and were considered of little account. But as their numbers grew there began to develop within the UN an 'African lobby'. Before important debates concerning Africa in the General Assembly and Security Council, members of African delegations would meet and agree on a common line.

The African lobby at the UN was a positive step. But the CPP government's ultimate objective of a united Africa would involve a single African vote in the UN. This would be more powerful than any number of votes from separate African states.

The Ghana government actively supported the peace-keeping work of the UN in the Congo between 1960 and 1964. Ghanaian troops formed part of the UN operation when Lumumba in 1960 appealed for military assistance after Moise Tshombe announced the secession of Katanga.

But having supported UN intervention, Ghanaian troops found themselves part of a UN force engaged in operations which resulted in the fall and consequent murder of Lumumba, the leader of the very government which had sought UN support.

The experience confirmed the CPP view that African solutions had to be found for African problems.

In 1963, the Ghanaian delegation at the UN discussed with the Africa Group a plan for an All-African force to be sent to the Congo.

The establishing of an All-African High Command to maintain peace in Africa instead of relying on outside forces such as the UN or NATO, remained a key objective of the Party.

The CPP and the Commonwealth

Ghana remained a member of the Commonwealth throughout the years of CPP government.

Ghana's role was key in the work of Commonwealth Conferences when African issues were discussed.

This became very apparent during the time of the crisis in (then) Rhodesia when it became clear in 1964 that the settler government was moving towards a unilateral declaration of independence (UDI).

At the 1965 Commonwealth Conference in London, African and Asian countries agreed a common line in opposing UDI. This was largely a result of Nkrumah's efforts. The Conference agreed that the principle of one man one vote should be applied to Rhodesia, and that there should be unimpeded progress to majority rule.

When in 1965 UDI was declared, the CPP government drew up proposals for joint action by African states to assist in the overthrow of the Ian Smith settler regime, and to go to the help of any African state attacked or threatened by it. In addition, Ghana indicated an intention to leave the Commonwealth.

The reputation of Ghana was further enhanced when largely owing to the efforts of Nkrumah, apartheid South Africa was forced to leave the Commonwealth. Ghana could not remain a member of an organisation containing the racialist minority government of South Africa. The British government had to choose between Ghana and South Africa. Britain chose Ghana. It was a measure of the stature of the CPP government. Britain knew that if Ghana left the Commonwealth, many African states would follow Ghana's lead.

Hanoi peace mission

Another important topic of the 1965 Commonwealth Conference was the war in Vietnam. A decision was taken to send a Commonwealth Commission to Hanoi. Nkrumah made preparations to lead it being the leader most acceptable to the Vietnamese.

Because of the continuance of the American bombing offensive, the Peace Mission had to be postponed. The Vietnamese leader Ho Chi Minh considered that Nkrumah's safety could not be assured.

It was not until February 1966 that the Americans agreed to halt bombing for a few days to allow Nkrumah's aircraft to land safely.

On 21 February 1966 Nkrumah boarded a VC10 of Ghana Airways at Accra airport to begin his journey to Hanoi. Before his departure he made a Will leaving all he had to the CPP, with the request that the Party would take care of his wife and three children.

He was never to see his family or his country again. His departure was the signal for a reactionary military/police coup to overthrow the CPP government.

5

CPP IS BANNED: THE CONAKRY YEARS 1966–72

End of CPP government

The military/police coup of 24 February 1966 was carried out by elements of army and police supported by foreign intelligence organisations and local groups opposed to the policies of the CPP.

For some hours the Presidential Guard Regiment at Flagstaff House resisted fiercely, but was eventually forced to surrender. There was no popular participation in the coup. The ordinary people were initially stunned.

Troops and police rounded up key CPP personnel and flung them into prison. Practically the entire Party leadership throughout the country was arrested. Included were all cabinet ministers, members of Parliament, officials of the CPP and all its subsidiary, associate organisations including trade union leaders.

With Nkrumah out of the country en route to Vietnam with peace proposals, with all the key points in Accra seized, and with the CPP leadership arrested, immediate effective resistance was out of the question.

A military/police junta installed itself in power, declaring the CPP government abolished and the Party banned.

Nkrumah was told the news when he arrived in Peking. He was by then well out of range of a quick return to Ghana. In the circumstances he decided to make an immediate statement to the Ghanaian people, and to fight back on African soil as soon as the necessary travel arrangements could be made.

The Party did not die on 24 February 1966.

It lived on in Conakry, Guinea where Nkrumah and his entourage stayed from 1966–72 at the invitation of President Sékou Touré and the PDG. It lived on underground in Ghana, surfacing from time to time under different party names. It remained alive in the CPP Overseas, and in the Diaspora. It lived and grew even stronger in the Pan-African Movement. For the reactionary coup in Ghana was not a domestic matter affecting only the people of Ghana. It was to have repercussions for the whole of the African people, on the continent and worldwide.

The Party and Nkrumaist response to the coup is summed up in the words of Nkrumah:

> *'One step backwards has been taken. We shall take two forward'.*

5 CPP is Banned: The Conakry Years 1966–72

Villa Syli, Conakry 1966–72

Nkrumah and his entourage arrived in Guinea on 2 March 1966 to a twenty-gun salute signalling to the world that Guinea still recognised Nkrumah as Ghana's head of state.

In an unprecedented expression of Pan-Africanism Nkrumah was appointed co-president of Guinea.

Villa Syli, Nkrumah's residence in Conakry, became the central point both for efforts to restore constitutional government in Ghana, and for the continuance of CPP Pan-African objectives.

The struggle was pursued through:

1. Organisation. The preparation of practical plans for a return to Ghana and the restoration of constitutional government.
2. Broadcasts to the people of Ghana by Nkrumah on Guinea's *Voice of the African Revolution*.
3. Close contacts with CPP support groups both inside Ghana, in the UK, in the Diaspora, throughout Africa and elsewhere.
4. Books, pamphlets and statements by Nkrumah. These were published by Panaf Books Ltd, a company established in the UK to publish and distribute the works of Nkrumah written in Guinea, and to keep in print those written before 1966. Neither of Nkrumah's previous UK publishers were willing to publish his writings after the fall of his government.
5. The magazine *Africa and the World*, a London based monthly magazine, founded in 1960 and

sponsored by the CPP government. It had a world-wide readership and a high reputation for progressive and accurate reporting. After the coup the magazine managed to continue publishing the truth about Ghana and Africa until 1971 when lack of funds forced it to close.

The life of Villa Syli was organised into a highly disciplined constructive unit, with each person equipping himself ideologically and physically for the arduous struggle ahead. Members of the entourage with security or police training joined Guinean security forces in protecting Villa Syli, screening visitors and so on. Those with secretarial skills attended to the work of Nkrumah's office, dealing with the vast number of cables, letters and messages of support which poured in from all parts of the world. Some were assigned the task of monitoring news broadcasts from Ghana and compiling daily reports for Nkrumah. Villa Syli had its own radio facilities which enabled official and secret communications between military and police sources to be heard. Other members of the entourage attended to ordinary household tasks.

A Political Committee was formed by members of Nkrumah's entourage, as part of a politicisation programme. Its first task was to examine the causes and aftermath of the coup in Ghana. What were the internal and external forces behind it? Where and how did the Party fail? What lessons could be learned?

5 CPP is Banned: The Conakry Years 1966-72

These were the questions being discussed among Party members in Ghana and elsewhere. How, when Ghanaians enjoyed one of the highest standards of living in Africa, could there have been sufficient Ghanaians, willing to collude with external forces determined to overthrow the CPP government? Why the defections of some key CPP officials? How was it that the Party's extensive programme of political education failed to prevent the coup?

The following were among some of the conclusions reached by the Political Committee:

1. The main external forces behind the coup were the Intelligence agencies of the USA, Britain and West Germany.
2. There were 'certain deficiencies' in the Party, its integral 'wings' and in the Civil Service, state corporations, armed forces and police. For example, there was mismanagement of some state farms, waste of equipment, inefficiency and lack of 'political orientation'.

Underlying most of the Political Committee's Report and recommendations for action on the Party's return to power was the need to stress the importance of educating the masses to know and understand the policies and methods of the CPP, necessary to build a society based on Pan-African socialist principles.

It was a lack of political awareness among the people and not any underlying fault of Party principles and policies.

CPP Overseas

Through meetings, demonstrations, seminars and so on, and their bulletin *The Dawn*, members of the Party in London showed their continuing loyalty to the CPP, refusing to accept the military junta's assertion that the Party was abolished.

The CPP Overseas issued a statement on the same day as the coup (24 February 1966), condemning the military action and pledging support for the constitutional government.

External Nkrumaist groupings

From 1966 onwards, Nkrumaists in Britain, Europe, throughout Africa and elsewhere formed organisations committed to the political philosophy of Nkrumah. Each claimed to be the authentic voice of Nkrumaism. But they differed in their interpretation of the term, what it implied, and also the procedures to follow. They spoke of 'Nkrumaism' rather than the 'CPP'.

Disunity of the various groups each claiming to be Nkrumaist was caused largely by lack of ideological clarity. Confusion concerning Nkrumaist parties which mushroomed in Ghana over the years was also a factor in continuing frustration and failure to unite.

5 CPP is Banned: The Conakry Years 1966-72

The Party and Pan-Africanism

While Nkrumah lived in Guinea, Villa Syli was both the external headquarters of the Party and a dynamic centre of Pan-Africanism.

The PDG government and the people of Guinea, diplomats of progressive African states such as Tanzania, Uganda and Zambia, members of the embassies of Vietnam, China, the USSR and North Korea were frequent visitors to Villa Syli. Freedom fighters, representatives of progressive organisations world-wide were as at home in Conakry as they had been in Accra during the time of the CPP government.

The main reason why Nkrumah and his supporters worked so tirelessly for a restoration of a CPP government in Ghana was to continue working towards the Party's Ghanaian and Pan-African goals.

The time factor was of vital importance.

If too much time elapsed before the return, the infrastructure which the CPP government had so carefully constructed, and which was necessary for the on-going struggle, might be irreparably damaged.

In Guinea, Nkrumah resolved that on his return to Ghana he would devote his time to organising the total liberation and unification of Africa, leaving the day to day administration of Ghana to the Party.

The death of Kwame Nkrumah

'The Greatest African', the words which Sékou Touré ordered to be inscribed on the coffin of Nkrumah, died at 8-45 am on 27 April 1972, in Bucharest, Romania. He had been unwell for some time but had refused to leave Guinea for medical treatment until August 1971.

On 30 April, three days after his death, Kwame Nkrumah returned to Africa. The Guinean government had arranged for his body to be preserved, placed in a special coffin and flown to Conakry.

For two days, on 13 and 14 May 1972, funeral ceremonies were held in Conakry, attended by representatives of liberation movements, governments, progressive parties and movements from Africa and elsewhere. Freedom fighter Amilcar Cabral in an Address which came to be known as 'The Cancer of Betrayal', expressed the determination of Africans:

> 'To succeed in the development of the economic, social and cultural progress of our peoples, and in the building of African unity; this was the fundamental objective of the actions and thought of Kwame Nkrumah; it is a vow to achieve this objective that we must all take before history and the African continent.'

On 7 July 1972, after weeks of negotiations between the Guinean government and the military regime in Ghana, the coffin of Kwame Nkrumah was flown to

5 CPP is Banned: The Conakry Years 1966–72

Accra. Flags flew at half mast while the coffin was lying-in-state at State House and a memorial service was held.

Then on 9 July it was taken to Nkroful where it was placed in a tomb on the site of his birthplace.

The final resting place of 'The Greatest African' and founder of the Convention People's Party, is in a marble mausoleum in a beautiful Memorial Park on the site of the Polo Ground in Accra, where Kwame Nkrumah declared the Independence of Ghana on 6 March 1957. The Re-interment ceremony took place on 1 July 1992, the thirty-second anniversary of the Republic of Ghana.

'Dark Days in Ghana'

This is the title of the first book which Nkrumah wrote in Conakry. In this book he exposed the true nature of the military/police regime in Ghana after the 1966 overthrow of constitutional government, and set it in the wider context of the African continent and world situation.

Few would argue with the words 'Dark Days' to describe conditions in Ghana in the post-1966 years, when progressive economic and social structures which the CPP government had so painstakingly built, were dismantled or allowed to disintegrate. Housing, education, health care, employment and other aspects of CPP Development Plans, all suffered. Ghana lost its position as pacemaker in Africa, and as the champion of freedom fighters and Pan-Africanists.

Over the years, Ghanaians were subjected to a succession of reactionary military coups, broken only by two short periods of so-called civilian government. It was an unprecedented time of political, economic and social instability, a sad new experience for Ghanaians after years of constitutional, progressive CPP rule.

6

CPP RENAISSANCE: ACHIEVING NKRUMAIST UNITY

Problems of Nkrumaist parties and groupings

Between 1966 when the CPP was banned, and 1999 the year of the Party's fiftieth birthday, the main problem faced by Nkrumaists was one of how to achieve a united Party. For Ghanaians of widely differing political views claimed to be Nkrumaists. It is testimony to the great achievements of the CPP government that so many wished to be associated with it. But their activities caused confusion and divisiveness.

Though the CPP is by tradition a mass party, it has clear principles and objectives which cannot be compromised. Therefore, those claiming to be Nkrumaists, yet do not understand or support CPP policies, do the Party serious damage. Nkrumaism and the CPP are inseparable.

While Nkrumah was alive there was continuity of leadership. From Party headquarters in Guinea, contact was kept with supporters in Ghana and with the Party overseas. In broadcasts to the people of Ghana, and through the books and pamphlets he wrote in Conakry, encouragement and clear directions were given, providing strategy and tactics for the ongoing struggle. 'Let Organisation be your watchword'.

In the circumstances of that time, with the Party banned, and oppressive regimes in power, Nkrumah urged supporters to 'stand firm' and to reorganise in secret. He was confident that 'the will of the broad masses will reassert itself'.

However, as time passed and there was no popular uprising to restore constitutional government; also no possibility of a fair election, attention turned to the organising of a counter-coup. It was a tactic alien to traditional Party practice, nevertheless deemed the only practical, realistic way to proceed in view of the time factor. Continuing misrule and mismanagement threatened to destroy the essential infrastructure built by the CPP for the continuance of the Party's Ghanaian and Pan-African objectives.

The death of Nkrumah in April 1972 left the Party leaderless, thereby further complicating efforts to unite. There was no obvious successor. New parties proliferated. Each claimed to be the true inheritor of the CPP. With the name 'CPP' still banned, parties chose names which meant little to a largely apathetic, disillusioned electorate. Voters will not support a party which is split.

Furthermore, the CPP image continued to suffer from the prolonged, massive western media campaign to discredit it. There was also a generation factor. The youth had not experienced CPP rule. Nor had they learned about the Party's achievements as part of their education. Many Nkrumaist youngsters questioned the presence in the Party of some of the 'old guard' whom they considered had let the Party down, or who had outdated ideas.

Then there was the effect of changing world conditions, the ending of the Cold War, the structural collapse of the Soviet Union, the widespread propaganda of the western media proclaiming the death of socialism, and the virtues of 'the market' or 'gobalism' (turbo-capitalism).

False dawns

On two occasions, hopes were briefly raised of a possible return to some kind of Nkrumaist administration.

1. On 13 January 1972 when the government of Dr Kofi Abrefa Busia was overthrown in a coup d'état led by General Ignatius Kutu Acheampong. Dr Busia (prime minister from 1969–72) and leader of the Progress Party, was inheritor of the traditional opposition to the CPP. His overthrow, therefore, was seen by some as an Nkrumaist victory. But neither Acheampong's National Redemption Council (NRC), nor the Supreme Military Council which followed, could

qualify as Nkrumaist. In a climate of mounting public discontent, Acheampong was removed from power in a palace coup on 5 July 1978, led by General F. W. K. Akuffo.

2. During the administration of President Hilla Limann, leader of the People's National Party (PNP) 1979–1981. President Limann owed his position to the veteran Nkrumaist Imoro Egala, who named him as suitable to lead the PNP when Egala could not be cleared from disqualification to lead himself.

President Limann, a distinguished academic and civil servant, lacked CPP credentials. Furthermore, when Flight Lieutenant J. J. Rawlings, head of the Armed Forces Revolutionary Council (AFRC) handed over power to Limann on 24 September 1979, he made it clear that the Limann Government was on probation.

On 31 December 1981, when Rawlings deemed the Limann government to have failed, he staged a second coup d'état removing him from power and installing the national Provisional Defence Council (PNDC). The PNDC proscribed all party politics until the General Election of 1992 when the National Defence Council (NDC), successor to the PNDC, was declared the winner.

It was an election in which the 'CPP' was still banned, and when parties which claimed the CPP inheritance made little impact, lacking unity, effective leadership and ideological clarity.

People's Convention Party (PCP)

After the 1992 elections a breakthrough towards Party unity came when five Nkrumaist parties resolved to work together. They were the:
— National Independent Party (NIP)
— People's Heritage Party (PHP)
— People's Party for Democracy and Development (PPDD)
— National Convention Party (NCP)
— People's National Convention (PNC) (sections)

The purpose of the PCP was declared to be the uniting of Nkrumaists to forge a 'new Convention People's Party as the legitimate Nkrumaist platform'.

The Party was committed to Nkrumaist policies in Ghanaian, foreign and Pan-African spheres. It declared support for the United Nations Organisation, the Organisation of African Unity (OAU) and for the Economic Community of West African states (ECOWAS): and adherence to the principle of positive neutrality in international relations.

The PCP was to be a vanguard organisation, leaving the door open for all Nkrumaists and CPP-based organisations to join.

The Great Alliance

In the lead up to the parliamentary and presidential elections of December 1996, Ghana's main opposition parties, the PCP and the NPP, joined forces in an historic agreement known as The Great Alliance to remove President Jerry Rawlings and the NDC from power.

In a joint communiqué in August 1996, the NPP representing the UP tradition and the PCP belonging to the CPP tradition, declared that the two had agreed 'on all essential aspects of the Alliance, including their partnership in government.' The Alliance presidential candidate was to be J. A. Kufuor, leader of the NPP.

To many it was an unnatural alliance doomed to failure. Others considered a united opposition the only hope of defeating the 15-year incumbency of Rawlings and the NDC.

From the start there were serious problems. The NPP, descended from the UP of Dr J.B. Danquah and Dr Busia, was by tradition conservative and capitalist; while the PCP, a grouping of parties committed to an Nkrumaist agenda, was socialist, except for the PNC of ex-President Hilla Limann.

Long-standing animosity between the parties of the Alliance, combined with disputes over constituencies, parliamentary candidates, and other sensitive matters, resulted in an extremely fragile partnership. The fact that by no means all members of the Alliance parties agreed with the arrangement further complicated the situation.

Questions arose as to whether it was a fundamentally hopeless task to weld together two such differing political movements into even a temporary electoral alliance. Would not the electorate be utterly confused? — especially when the Great Alliance

6 CPP Renaissance: Achieving Nkrumaist Unity

lacked any clear programme apart from the negative objective of defeating the NDC. How could the PCP and the NPP hope to form a joint government if they won the election?

It was no surprise when in December 1996, the NDC once again was able to claim victory in both the parliamentary and presidential elections.

Memorandum of Understanding

On 16 October 1997, the unity of Nkrumaist political parties was pledged in a 'Memorandum and Communiqué' issued by the Supreme Council of Elders of the Nkrumah Political family, the PCP, NCP and PNC. Its purpose was to reaffirm the indivisibility of the CPP and to restore and rebuild the Party.

A Working Committee was set up to arrange a joint National Congress, when the name and symbol of the Party would be decided. The Parties adopted the Supreme Council of Elders, under the joint chairmanship of Dr Hilla Limann and Mr Kojo Botsio as a facilitating and mediating body for the Working Committee.

Campaign to unban the CPP

Resistance to the banning of the CPP dates back to the February 1966 coup when the CPP government was overthrown and all political activity banned.

For many years, while military regimes were in power, opposition to the ban had to be covert. Later, when political activity was permitted, attempts were openly made to get the ban on the CPP lifted. The matter was pursued through the Ghana judiciary, but without success. Nevertheless, Nkrumaists in Ghana and overseas continued to work tirelessly, organising pressure groups, appeals, demonstrations, petitions and so on. It was a campaign destined never to end until victory, when Nkrumaists could once again gather under the banner of the 'CPP', the historic Party name indelibly imprinted in the minds of all true Nkrumaists.

The Convention Party (CP)

In 1998, with parliamentary and presidential elections due to take place in December 2000, it was essential to register a CPP party without further delay, to allow sufficient time to organise an efficient election campaign. If the 'CPP' could not be registered, then the nearest equivalent had to be chosen.

The Convention Party was born on 11 August 1998 when the Party received its final certificate of registration from the Electoral Commission. In the words of an Nkrumaist: 'The CP *is* the CPP'.

It was the mainstream Nkrumaist formation, comprising the PHP, NIP, PPDD, the Nkrumaist Caucus, NCP, and sections of the PNC.

The Party retained the cockerel symbol of the CPP, and its motto: *FORWARD EVER, BACKWARD NEVER*.

CP political structures were put in place at national, regional, constituency and ward levels. Interim officers were appointed to carry on the work of the

6 CPP Renaissance: Achieving Nkrumaist Unity

Party until the calling of a National Congress, when finishing touches would be would be put in place for a party programme of mass mobilisation.

The experienced CPP veteran, Comrade Kojo Botsio was appointed Interim Chairman of the Party.

Impetus for the merger of Nkrumaist forces which resulted in the formation of the CP, had come from the grassroots, notably from the youth. This augured well for the future, as did the CP's clearly stated adoption of Nkrumaism as its political philosophy. Henceforth, no person or organisation dishonestly claiming to be Nkrumaist could have any credence. Actions speak louder than words. Self-called Nkrumaists, whose actions expose them as bogus, could no longer cause confusion or pose a threat.

'The Convention'

Soon after the birth of the CP, the Party newspaper *The Convention* was launched in Accra. By publicising the policies and work of the CP the newspaper was to mobilise and politically educate the masses of Ghana in support of the Party's political, social, economic and Pan-African objectives.

'Commitment journalism' was to be the cornerstone of editorial policy. In this respect, *The Convention* fitted into the Nkrumaist tradition, being reminiscent of the *Accra Evening News*, founded by Osagyefo Kwame Nkrumah in 1948, which was the mouthpiece of the CPP, and which played such an important role in galvanising mass support for the Independence struggle.

Similarly, *The Convention* was to provide essential media coverage and support for the CP in the campaign to win the parliamentary and presidential elections of December 2000.

Fiftieth birthday of the CPP: 12th June 1999

In the history of every country there are landmark dates marking decisive turning points. Landmark dates in Ghana's history are all connected with the CPP.

12 June 1949	Birth of the CPP
6 March 1957	Independence
I July 1960	Republic Day
24 February 1966	Re-Dedication Day
12 June 1999	50th birthday of the CPP

Party Calendar

24 February	Re-Dedication Day
6 March	Independence Day
27 April	Founder's death
12 June	Party's anniversary
1 July	Republic Day
21 September	Founder's birthday

Books by Kwame Nkrumah

Year of
Publication

1945   *Towards Colonial Freedom*

1957   *Autobiography*
'To my Mother"

1961   *I Speak of Freedom*
'Dedicated to Patrice Lumumba, late Prime Minister of the Republic of the Congo, and to all those who are engaged in the struggle for the political unification of Africa.'

1963   *Africa Must Unite*
'Dedicated to George Padmore (1900–1959), and to the African nation that must be'.

1964   *Consciencism: Philosophy and Ideology for Decolonisation*

1965   *Neo-Colonialism: The Last Stage of Imperialism*
'This book is dedicated to the Freedom Fighters of Africa living and dead.'

1966   *Challenge of the Congo: A Case Study of Foreign Pressures in an Independent State*
'A Ahmed Sékou Touré, Mon Frère de Combat Au Bureau Politique national du Parti Démocratique de Guinée, et au Vaillant Peuple de Guinée, Aux Peuples Africains et aux Courageux Militants pour la Cause Sacrée du progrès Africain dans la Liberté et l'Unité du Continent'.

1966	*Axioms: Freedom Fighters Edition*
1967	*Voice from Conakry*
1968	*Dark Days in Ghana* 'To Major General Barwah, Lieutenant S. Arthur and Lieutenant M. Yeboah and all Ghanaians killed and injured resisting the traitors of the 24th February 1966'.
1968	*Handbook of Revolutionary Warfare: A Guide to the Armed Phase of the African Revolution* 'To the African guerrilla.'
1968	*Ghana: The Way Out* (Pamphlet)
	The Spectre of Black Power (Pamphlet)
	The Struggle Continues (Pamphlet)
1969	*Two Myths* (Pamphlet)
	The Big Lie (Pamphlet)
1970	Revised edition of *Consciencism*
1970	*Class Struggle in Africa* 'This book is dedicated to the workers and peasants of Africa'.

Published posthumously

1973	*The Struggle Continues* (Contains the 5 pamphlets written in Conakry 1968/9, and *What I Mean by Positive Action* written in Accra in 1949)
	Revolutionary Path
1974	*Rhodesia File*

6 CPP Renaissance: Achieving Nkrumaist Unity

Chronology

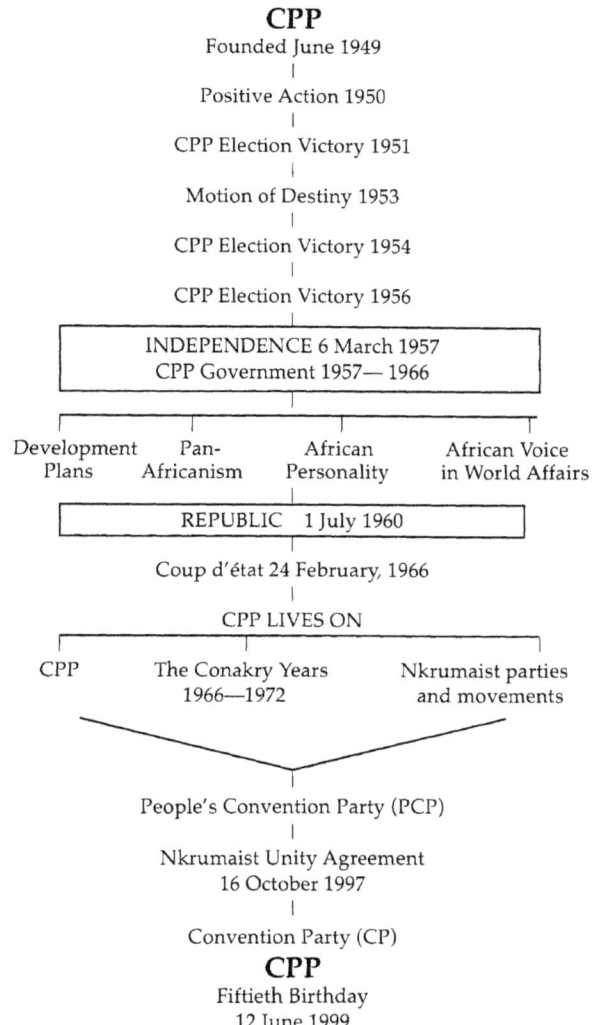

www.ingramcontent.com/pod-product-compliance
Lightning Source LLC
Chambersburg PA
CBHW070309240426
43663CB00039BA/2555